Nude as F***

Copyright © 2025 by Monique Rebellion Jones.

All rights reserved. No part of this book may be reproduced in any form or by any electronic or mechanical means, including information storage and retrieval systems, without permission in writing from the publisher, except by reviewers, who may quote brief passages in a review.

This publication contains the opinions and ideas of its author. It is intended to provide helpful and informative material on the subjects addressed in the publication. The author and publisher specifically disclaim all responsibility for any liability, loss, or risk, personal or otherwise, which is incurred as a consequence, directly or indirectly, of the use and application of any of the contents of this book.

MILTON & HUGO L.L.C.
4407 Park Ave., Suite 5
Union City, NJ 07087, USA

Website: www.miltonandhugo.com
Hotline: 1- 888-778-0033
Email: info@miltonandhugo.com

Ordering Information:
Quantity sales. Special discounts are available on quantity purchases by corporations, associations, and others. For details, contact the publisher at the address above.

Library of Congress Control Number:	2025931371
ISBN-13: 979-8-89285-297-5	[Paperback Edition]
979-8-89285-296-8	[Digital Edition]

Rev. date: 02/05/2025

I dedicate this book to God, my soul provider, source of my existence. You have prepared me to enjoy this life no matter the circumstances, fear, or worldly destruction. God, thank you for gradually making me conscious of my behavior as I evolve.

God has given me the strength to live long enough to write this version of my heart. Thank you for creating my mother and father in this walk of life. I made this for you God. I made this so you know I won't ever give up on the vision you have given me. I truly love you, and I know I will never be enough for flesh on earth, I just pray I am what you designed me to be.

To my family, thank you for encouraging me,
and pushing me forward in your own way.

To Sagira and Ezekiel, thank you for
showing me God's strength.

To my husband, thank you for being a giant and
putting me in places that reflected us.

To Maurice, thank you for going on this journey
with me and illustrating my words.

To the reader, thank you for choosing this book and fixing your eyes to read, your mind to understand, your heart to feel me, and your earnings to exchange energy. Thank you for seeing me.

Triple R Solutions
By Monique Rebellion Jones

Chapters

Death 1
The Resistance 10
Solitude 20
Growth 30
The Rebirth 48
Process 57
Living Inside 66
NUDE AS F*** 73

The dirt filled my finger tips
I couldn't recognize my own hand.
I could not see the scene from your view.
I could only see the hand... my hand.
The dirt...
I could only feel... the hurt.
Heavy was the weight of my enemies weapon
They have murdered me.
They have left me for death.
What could I have done
to lay under the hands
of a friend?
They spoke words of jealousy
They stole my vision and used their false relationships
to generate my operation.
It seems they have destroyed me.
Now, I lie here in the dirt.

Wait...
What's that smell?
It's sweet, it's spicy...
It smells like... an opportunity.
I have to get up.
I have to become, I have to be.
I am still me, I think...
I feel, I know, What I will become...
What is in this dirt?
How will it support my growth?
I have to become, I have to be.
I don't recognize what was anymore,
Yet, I know who I am for sure.

I HAVE BEEN DESPERATE FOR YOUR EYE GAZE.
I HAVE BEEN DESPERATE FOR YOUR HELP.
I HAVE BEEN DESPERATE FOR YOU TO JOIN ME IN THIS PROCESS.
I HANG ONTO EVERY WORD YOU SAY. I AM SURE I AM YOUR DAUGHTER.
WE LAUGH THE SAME, SMILE THE SAME, WALK THE SAME,
I THINK.
WHERE HAVE YOU BEEN?
I THOUGHT SHE WAS IN BETWEEN OUR GROWTH. . .
BUT IT SEEMS ONLY THREATS BY DEATH BRING YOU NEAR.
IF YOU ARE SO AFRAID OF LOSING ME, WHY HAVE YOU TURNED INTO FEAR?
WHY HAVE YOU EASED INTO ANOTHER STORY LINE WITHOUT ME. . . AGAIN?
WHEN YOU FOUND US, HOW COME YOU DIDN'T GET ON THAT BUS AND COME TO US?
I HAVE BEEN DESPERATE FOR YOUR HAND.
I WAS SO AFRAID EVERYONE WOULD BE JUST LIKE YOU,
SLIPPING THROUGH MY FINGERS LIKE QUICK SAND.
I AM STILL HOPING FOR THE DAY WHERE YOU COULD SHOW ME YOUR BEAUTY.
MAYBE, THEN, I WILL SEE HOW BEAUTIFUL YOU INTENDED FOR ME TO BE.
I SEE YOU AS MY CREATOR IN THE FLESH, BUT JUST THE KING JAMES VERSION;
        HOPING MY STRENGTH WOULD BE THE DIVERSION.
I USED TO CONSIDER MY GOD MADE A MISTAKE, WHEN HE MADE ME.
I HAVE BEEN DESPERATE TO PROVE TO YOU, I AM WORTHY OF YOUR PRESENCE.
I AM WORTHY OF YOUR LOVE.
I HAVE FOCUSED IN THEIR SYSTEM, SURPASSED YOU IN YOUR WORKS,
I HAVE REGENERATED FOR YOU.
I HAVE MULTIPLIED YOUR FACE ON THIS EARTH SPACE. . .
YET, STILL YOUR LOVE IS LIMITED. . . BLOCKED BY A WALL OF SHAME.
HAVE YOU YET TO HEAL WHAT YOU REFUSE TO REVEAL?
WILL I HAVE TO DO THIS ALL ON MY OWN?
WILL I HAVE TO BE RICH, TO TAKE YOU IN. . . AND SHOW YOU MY LOVE.
SOMETIMES, I AM DESPERATE FOR YOUR HUGS.
DESPERATE FOR THE IDEA OF COMPLETENESS.
DYING FOR MY DAD'S LOVE.

I died today.
It was no ordinary death.
It was like any other day, when I took a deep breath.
And there I was, standing before my lifeless body.
I wish I could have said, I was sad about it.
I wish I could say I was relieved.
Instead, I felt nothing.
Finally, all of my questions about my existence
were taking place in this one instance.
I recognized the distance,
then I got persistent.
I finally skipped ahead, to the moment when I really was dead.
I was like a battery that could not be stored into a freezer for recharge.
I disintegrated into my vision
I had prayed and wished for death to come.
I agonized over this shell, and the many shells that made being. . .
Women. . . difficult. . .
That made being. . .
Native American difficult. . .
That made being me. . . difficult.
Until I realized I still existed beyond the labels,
The titles, the status quo, or even my own narrative.
I realized that death has been my destiny.
My story has ended.
No more chapters, no more interludes, no more concepts,
No more trying. . .
Just death.
Just observing my lifeless body, and recalling all that I have done,
All that u could have done, and all that I was no longer controlling.
Wow, who knew that I could be a deadass, living in my regrets.
Death seemed to have been way worse than living.
I suppose, in this construct, I will enjoy death as much as I wished I
would have. . . The living.

Could we scream until our last breath.
Experience prana stripping itself from this sheath.
Form an alliance with pain and bring it some pleasure.
Construct a conscious experience.
We could call it Faith deliverance.
I AM being ser–ious.
From the elites creating infrastructures
To deconstruct joy
–To– illuminated minds destructing our genetic connection
To source,
I am beginning to feel like Beetlejuice.
Say my name
Say his name
Say their name
Say our name...
As my brothers and sisters names are consciously spread
We unconsciously cope with the oppressors tools
Boxing ourselves into threads of systems cupped with confusion.
When will we acknowledge that we agreed to this illusion of salvation...
For it is better than fighting injustice in a court of educated bigots,
Or riot to be heard
Or rebel against the grain for our parental figures to trust their vision seeded in us.
Could we scream until we have an effective solution?
Could we agree that capitalism is a never ending division?
Could we agree abortion, distortion and redundant racial threats...
Are consciously destroying our ability to evolve.
Or would agreeing to unification destroy the strong, by passing the torch to the weak.

It is an assumption, but we must agree that disagreeing is not a solution... It may very well be the diversion to the death of history—

One blow to the head
I'm not dead
I'm alive
To be born again.
To arrive again.

One blow to the head
I'm not dead
I'm alive
To be born again
To arise again

One blow to the head
Face on the concrete
Organs exposed
How could I not see?
Maybe my reality was misconstrued
With fairytales
Of being the one, one, one
Who's you?

One blow to the head
I'm not dead
I'm alive
To be born again

To ARISE again.

Too many times we've been criminalized
Dehumanized
Into a matter that depends on it.
I shape shift my fears
And I spin on it.

"Inches into the ground, and still the trees have more authority over..."

If I had a moment to talk to the devil in anyone,
I would tell them to love more.
To abandon their misery
To abandon the temporary satisfaction of existing in their grief.
I would tell them to stop exploring the hate from the past
To eliminate the desire to make hate last.
Shit, I talk to the devil in me
& tell that hating ass bitch to set herself free
There's too much Holy will power in me
To just let fear swallow me whole
I stepped up to the plate
Acknowledged everything that I hate
I'm at peace
I switched my fear to Faith
Living by the principal
Living to be sensible
I'm at peace...
Yet there's a piece of me...
Captured in the "what will this life make of me?"
What will become of me?
Making decisions that are radical.
Believing the voice in my head telling me...
I should be dead, or to kill everyone ahead...
Or expose myself to the nothingness,
Become obsessed by the light.
Somehow put up a fight.
Death passed quicker through my canal than life did
It made me wonder into my shadows
It made me question my light
I swallowed my decision
I cried and mourned (I heard strength boasting in the background)

Push, Push, Push
Push back, never hold back
Release it all into the hands of another
Until you're a mother
Push, Push, Push
your tears into your palm,
Go read your psalms
Never let another know your doubt has grown
"Push, Push, Push,
Your loved one's away"
That's what my inner demon would say
Then I would go run away
And stay
Far from the light
Oh how it shines and exposes my critters
I've been patient
I've been meek
I've been compassionate
Until a friend said "what about me?"
I respond, what about me?
I enjoy pushing things away
It shows my strength
Yet, I insisted, cowardly
I needed to return to the light within me
Solar Eclipse
Mood continues to dip
Vibration shrinking by the minute
I just pray, I don't go preying on another
Smiling and cheerful they are. . .
I try to step into the light, but the first thing I see is a scar
"Oh, why, why am I the way that I are"
28 YEARS later, I'm standing on a cliff
Then I realize everything in the dark remains the same
I gutted my scars and dragged out shame. . . into the light.

A pack of Newport a day since her lover ran away,
He was only sixteen years old on earth.
He wanted to touch a star,
No matter how far,
But she enjoyed her heels on the ground.
She fancied the way his eyes stayed off of her.
It was her challenge to change a man:
To make him gaze her way, and say here I am.
Yet, he couldn't quell the sound of her voice.
He'd lay cautiously in her bed with his headphones blanketing his
Ears while blasting MF DOOM in her apartment bedroom.
She would cry a river to make him flow away
She threw rocks and stones,
But he wore them as chains
Then, the fall had come
And she had grew flowers
He looked back, and tried to return
Then, suddenly he saw the stars that surrounded her,
But it was too late
The stones overturned his gaze
Her mind shifted his labyrinth
Before she knew it,
Her stars followed him..
All along
If she would have built a boat for the river she cried
She would find her float
And who knows, they would've grown into the stars they've known.

Every compliment leads with a smile.
I resisted, and questioned it with a frown.
Every gift leads with genuine pleasure.
I resisted, and questioned, to what measure?
Sometimes, the fragile souls lead to a place
Where? No one genuinely knows.
Naïve, was innocent.
Naïve, was the child.
Naïve, was the mother.
Naïve, but no one questioned the criminal
Who knew that being naïve was the one who questioned no one.
Naïve, was the son.
His logic wrapped around impulse,
But the criminal who cracked open his mind. . .
Was yet to be special, nor one of a kind.
Naïve, was the banker.
Naïve was the African chief.
Naïve, was the land.
Naïve, unlike the waters.
A flow into the sand
A structure uneven into the cement.
A flow into the roots of a tree.
A structure into the pipes of a building.
No one knows, until they experience control.
I resisted to believe that no one truly knows.

> "Once a butterfly ate too much junk, therefore, it grew mold around its cocoon. It is built to fly, so it escaped with new eyes."
> — Monique Rebel Jones —

Hi my name is
Rebellion with a cause and effect.
Hi my name is Renaissance with a cause and effect.
Hi my name is Riot with a cause and effect.
Hi my name is Journey with a cause and effect.
Hi my name is. . .
I think my name is. . .
They called our my name for a month..
Then another right after.
We were piling up. . .
No pictures thereafter.
Hi my name is. . .
I forgot.. Over the tears. . . It's a lot.
Hi my name is. . .
That woman who was hung in a cell
Please do tell. . .
My brothers and my sisters over in Asia
Somewhere in the water is a memory of lost names.
I hope the world remember me, like they remember that entertainer
What do they call her?
Oh, Queen B.
Hi, my name is consumer with a cause and effect.
Hi my name is capitalism with a cause and effect.
Hi my name is Radical with a cause and effect.
Hi my name is bullet, with a cause and effect.

There's more to life than holding on to things,
More like holding on to people.
We all want to be safe, but we need something to be safe from.
So as long as we feel unsafe, life will be worth fighting for. . .
Said, "Hi. My name is resistance".

Thanks to your self doubt,
You, bought into their product.
Now you lucubrate your illusions,
Pondering on what will happen when you
Come to face your number 8.
You know,
Things don't ever stay the same
Even through time and space
Changes pace.
No time, for animosity towards,
The reason you held back.
No time for blame,
You've already shamed that...
Come on,
Get up.
Move on,
Move forward.
You're dreams aren't real
Until you heal, by moving forward.
Wish you could.
Wish you would've?
But what about tomorrow,
When you realized,
You really should've...
Give it another try
Don't say you couldn't even if they lie.
They gon push on the way up..
They gon stomp on the way down.
Just think of it as Black Friday at the TV store...
Where the TV sellers are even poorer than the landlord.

"To start a new cycle, it will require a new seed."

— Rebel Monique Jones —

Patterns of pain
Creates the intention of suffering.
Where there is constant pressure,
There appears, constant strain.

I know pain.
I know the fear of failing before starting.
I know pain before pain could introduce itself to me.
I know pain.

I know what it is like to choose the worst possibility,
before
Choosing the best.

Pain traumatized me with desirable outcomes,
Turning into flames.
I know pain.

It is pressure on our heads,
Like gravity
It pushes in a downward motion.

Like birthing a human through
The pillars of pleasure.

What she doesn't know,
she feared it so much,
She chose pain instead of pushing for pleasure.

The scar of pain
Appears as a reminder to always choose
My own destiny, and not fear.

It is suspected that my time alone,
Is physically without sound.
Instead, I need to be absent of others,
To enjoy the company of those I have adopted...
From books,
From television,
From pain,
From my misconceptions,
From the Cartesian theater that entertain my ego...

To be quiet in a room full of people
Is to be an observant loner.

I miss the absence of myself.
As I sit quietly listening to the sounds of
Cups meeting the floating surface
Or
The brewing of coffee clashing with the blues
Bumping out of the large projector.

Empty rooms are not made for solitude.
As I am searching for the emptiness in me,
that exempts my ego from the controlled narrative
I expand my external existence.
For once, I am being exactly as I am made to exist.
Individual impulse identity, to be.
Bridging innocence and wisdom
Over the seas of experimental behavior.
I am, the ether.

I wish I was stronger to let you know,
There are multiple ways to love.

Somehow when all alone in this empty room
I close my eyes, and I perceive your face in the corners of my mind.
I go from gloom, to cherry blossom bloom.

Clutter is my prefrontal lobe
Decisions, decisions.
When will I make the decision to release the pressure?
When will the pressure expand into strength?

How much more support will I receive when I begin the journey within?
How many cycles will I need to shed skin?

I accept the story I am given,
I push my pen,
No filter to push out
What was once in,
No plastic,
But I bottle the juice
I embody abundance
I am profuse in everything I do.

I do it single handedly
No scandal.

I wanna feel my tongue on your
Clitoris
He said,
"I want to put the tip all the way in"
He said,
With his freshly manicure, scrolling my vulva.
Yes, I was sure he was ready to enter my world.
So, I disrobed my curves.
I slipped then he swerved
I ringed every nerve.
Now, our bodies are reacting to his stories.
I was the main character in his episodes.
All in the privacy of my own Cartesian theater,
He was attentive to every meter.
Scented fire around the bed.
Inflammable, I was, before I tasted the head.
Imagination never tasted so good,
But was I imagining this, or was I recalling lifting the hood?
He squeezed me between his lips.
My pillars remained sturdy
It was not as though he did not make me collapse.
But after a leg day, I was not going to relapse.
So I gripped the 1,000 thread of cotton sheets
Unintentionally, digging my finger tips in each square thread.
This man was about to kill me in my own bed.
Devour me every minute before the climax hour.
I wanted him to. . .
I want him more than I want oxygen. . .
That is what the rose would have to do. . .
His t-shirt would have to do. . .
His scent would have to do. . .
His smile and mustache engraved in my memory would have to bring me to orgasmic bloom.

Solitude

"Growing pains, looks beautiful externally,
And I plant seeds to love you eternally."

— Rebel Monique Jones —

(3/2023 My husband returns from Military Training)
Solid in my shell.
Solid I prevail.
All this hell.
All this pain.
All of this will help me gain,
Because I am a beautiful woman.
I'm a soft woman.
I'm a gentle woman.
Don't let me become anything else, I say to myself
"I could really be better."
"I could really be stronger."
I could really care for you. . .

I like to be alone.
All alone in my apartment,
As I compartmentalize
The trauma, and the self inflicted stress of being broke,
Horny.
Conservatively liberal about being black.

Nothing to do,
But, it wouldn't be me if I didn't find something to do.
Being busy is how I like to be,
When I am alone.
I tried binge watching my old favorite films, with elaborative sex scenes
which led me to my rose.
Rarely ever stroking on my back
Control freak!
And I enjoyed myself.
Because I realize I can not, will not
Spend my days only thinking about
My favorite enemy. . . time.
Neurons fire in my amygdala as I attempt to face the present day.

Every moment, I wheel (will) myself into courage,
I separate myself from fear.
Neurons somatically making gestures
As my current image is tucked away.
I accomplish my goals
As though I would obtain the wealth promised
If I am being blatantly honest,
I do not trust a promise.

My memories demand of me to shape a new mold.
So, I will give myself grace to unfold.

Memories of loss,
Reminds me of my avoidant dismissive attachments.
Attached.
Attached to things and people I haven't even met yet.
Existing in situations that would dissolve
My enthusiasm?
More like the adrenalin
Causing my heart to have spasms.
Blacking out when I am exactly where I want to be.
Eyes wide open, but my mind's eyes are afraid of what is meant to be.
Eyes wide shut.
Pineal Gland sprouting.
Painful?
No. But for you, I would not doubt it.
Hearing the beauty of a child prayers coming true,
We could force the cornea to see the sky as clear blue.
Yet, the Neurons in my amygdala
Fire off into the past. . . As I write. . . In my solitude.
I breathe to stretch the hope of
The greatest possibility.
Exhale and release the tension building from what was.

SHOULDERS COLLAPSING EVENLY
CORE STRONG AND FIRM
PELVIC BLENDING
LIKE A PAINT BRUSH ON A CANVAS BETWEEN MATTERS OF HUES...
I CHOOSE ME.
I CHOOSE TO MAKE MYSELF SMILE,
CONTAGIOUSLY.
COURAGEOUSLY,
I SMILE WHEN I AM DENIED,
I SMILE WHEN I AM UNDERESTIMATED.
THE ONLY DOUBTFUL PERSON RESPONSIBLE FOR MY GROWTH,
IS, I.
MY DNA DOES NOT CONTROL MY BEHAVIOR.
MY BEHAVIOR CONTROLS MY DNA.

I CHOOSE ME.
I CHOOSE TO MAKE MYSELF SMILE.
I CHOOSE TO BE CONTAGIOUS IN MY JOY, AND IN MY PRIDE.
I AM A PROUD EARTH BEING.
GROUNDED AND GOVERNED BY THE ELEMENTS.
I AM GROUNDED IN KNOWING THAT ALL
WORKS FOR MY BEST AND HIGHEST INTEREST.

Hairs on my right leg rise.
Ms. Harvey said, girl you are the prize.
But, his package holds something valuable
His poison is soluble, in. . .
My. . .
Mouth.
It is as though I am holding every possibility of his lineage
In my left hand,
This is a scrimmage
I am imagining him and I in an image
How deeply can I absorb the extension of his power?
Maybe, I could absorb better in the shower.
As I kneel into submission
I accept the steaming hot water into my follicles
It falls over my eyelids, making it easier to glide
Down my tongue
On his shaft
OUI baby, I know you're bad,
Fill my tonsils with your liquid gold
I'd rather procreate,
But I would just hate
To not be in this position
On a soft, yet sturdy knee.
I would just fall apart
If I couldn't feel your tender chocolate
Snicker
. . ..
I would just fall into abyss
Waiting in my solitude
For this to be reality. . .
Because now I'm kneeling in this shower,
With a plastic figure in my mouth.

Fatal attraction, deep diving in my womb
Honeycomb loving, medicinal
Your kindness adds to my cup.
You know wassup,
I just landed in Chicago, Wherever I go, you
Go.
My love is sweet, once you get past the hard
Side of me.
I know you would like to think, my behavior
Isn't called for,
But ever since I picked up the phone to
Heartbreak,
I was left with a lifestyle of heartache.

Touched down in Miami, looking for fun,
But it's no fun without you.

Touched down in LA, for a new persona
Just got off the phone with your momma,
She said, "Queen, you're the main
character..."

Yet, there's no plot without my love
Interests.
Even when we're at odds, we always balance
Ourselves out.
Palm trees aren't the same without the
Future in your eyes,
They all say leave him in the dust, but that
Just wouldn't be us.

"Developing the self to be sufficient,
is essential to our journey."

— Monique Rebel Jones —

Heart beat pumping anxiety through the left breast,
Looking at a reflection through the right eye
Contemplating is this the first stage before eye die

All alone in the skull
Yet, so many at the table.
All these voices are just sound waves.
A simple cell has been so dedicated to being loved.
Run away when love seems to test the boundaries.

Open up.
Open Up.
Open up,
Open.

If I knew how far time could go,
I would spend more time growing
Rather than sewing comparisons.

Threads of embarrassment,
Often times leaving surrogates
Injected with a frame of mind
One in which dimensions
Does not fit mine.

Some memories recall it as a lesson of growth.
Still in my body
I know better than the collective will admit.

Despised how each of us could afloat.
Oh, how this vehicle of a body could turn adversity into love.

P.S.
Consciousness

He never put her in first place.
He never had her, in the first place.

He just collected ideas
Out of what he feared
He didn't consider her tears
    Except when he realized. . .
He never had her in the first place.

She kept her distance
& he kept her power

She kept getting angry,
He kept her feelings out of place.
24 hours, no emotion.
Gone without a trace.
Who are you going to follow that isn't hollow?
She nah fi hide under di makeup
Like di love is made up
No program would pick ha' up
No channel to predict her story— —

Then, she realized
He never put her in first place. . .

It's a fairy tale to think I am special to you
But your just a collector
You're not my protector
Your just a talker
Could you really walk the mile
Keep a smile
Is that what you really want?
If it's something, something
Please don't tell me nothing
Nothing....
From the womb to her arms
She cursed me
She was mad at the other part of me that reminded her how not to be cursed I thought
Cursed I thought I was, because I looked like the man Who planted the seed in her womb
Cursed I thought I was
Because I wasn't anything like she thought I would be
I was better
I didn't know it until 23
I broke the shackles off my knees
Started climbing mountains of 33 degrees
Wind blowing, but like a Capricorn
I keep my horns facing north
Rising
Doing doubles catching triples in degrees
That's how I set myself free
Could be blinding
Mommy gave me less hugs when my sibling was born
I didn't notice because I gave my sibling more

Tango in the living room
Dim lights but our spirits bloom.
Empty rooms,
But filled with sound
Empty rooms,
Filled with furniture.

Each piece of furniture
Personified in likeness to
The extremities of discomfort

Squeaky plastic to cover the tough fabric
What is comfortable,
If the bare minimum doesn't average?

What was ever the point of sacrificing your needs
Why would you always bury the seeds?

You can be alone in your misery,
Or you can live.

Turning opposition adjacent to my wins
Mirror my rough times
Transform the darkness within
Real love
Always meeting your needs
Sharing tools
So you can plant and water your seeds
Abandon the fools.
Stepping out my box
To reconfigure my paradox
Recognized that I am the key
Call me Mrs. Locke
Tik Tok as you wind down your misery
Almost lost my life
And still the devil couldn't get the best of me

Yea we swing
Back and forth
My twin flame
Eliminates the shame
As I learn to win the game
While you all just playing for the fame
I'm in the board house
Learning the labyrinth
That turn the Jedi Sith

SOMETHING IN YOUR PATH,
GOT YOU HAUNTED
SOMETHING IN THE THE PAST
SOMETHING THAT DIDN'T LAST
THERE IS ALWAYS SOMETHING,
SOMETHING

SOMETHING ABOUT THE WAY YOU
LINGER IN MY PSYCHE
I THINK THIS MIGHT BE,
SERIOUS!

THEN YOU DO SOMETHING,
SOMETHING
THAT LETS ME KNOW YOU'VE BEEN WITH SOMETHING
AND ALL OF ME, TO YOU, AMOUNTS TO NOTHING
BECAUSE YOU HAVE IT WITH EVERYONE

IT'S A FAIRY TALE TO THINK I AM SPECIAL TO YOU
BUT YOUR JUST A COLLECTOR
YOU'RE NOT MY PROTECTOR
YOUR JUST A TALKER
COULD YOU REALLY WALK THE MILE
KEEP A SMILE
IS THAT WHAT YOU REALLY WANT?

IF IT'S SOMETHING, SOMETHING
PLEASE DON'T TELL ME NOTHING
NOTHING. . . .

From the womb to her arms
She cursed me
She was mad at the other part of me that reminded her how not to be.
Cursed I thought.

Cursed I thought I was, because I looked like the man,
Who planted the seed in her womb.

Cursed I thought I was
Because I wasn't anything like she thought I would be
I was better
I didn't know it until 23
I broke the shackles off my knees
Started climbing mountains of 33
degrees
Wind blowing, but like a Capricorn
I keep my horns facing north,
Rising
Doing doubles catching triples in degrees
That's how I set myself free
Could be blinding
Momma gave me less hugs when my sibling was born
I didn't notice because I loved my sibling more
Then I realized the weight of my mothers heart became my own
I wasn't living life until I was living my own

Right now, I wish my mother would hug me
Hug me tight
...These are the words I write
To get me right...
When I'm lost in my head...
Lying down in my bed
Laying in the puddle of my tears
This is my Solitude.

Left foot to the right,
Right foot swings around
Twirling with red wine in my plastic cup
You know, wassup?.

The moments we shared,
Play on the projector of my mind.
  Zoomed into your face, looking for
Happiness and satisfaction.

Not another lesson I think to myself,
Sip.
Not another season filled with reasons.
Sip.
Not another loss for a grand gain I am uncertain I could carry.
Sip, sip, Guzzle.

How did we get here?
Were you ever in-love with me?
I tried to coordinate my appearance,
But it appears to be,
  None of your business.
Pour, splash,
Sip, pour, sip.

I just have to know. . ..Was it all for show?
Toxic optimism has brought me to my knees.
Am I CRAZY?
Or Am I in this wine bottle,
Oui ! that's my song
The one about the thong,
Oui! Oldies but goodies, and still feel you linger
In every imagination as I create. . .

Just give me peace.
He charmed me with his eyes
His afro stands firmly with loose ends spiraling in my direction.
His presence is enticing, but I'd rather be with myself.
I'd rather bring out my rose, and fuck myself until the sun rise
Than to operate in adultery,
I would rather go in the room, and listen to love songs before I
…

Before I lay with his vanilla glazed skin,
Why is the love I desire always wrapped in sin?

Potential is standing in quicksand.

"Self–love is a responsibility a parent has passed down. One must learn to pivot through the languages of love."

— Monique Rebel Jones —

Lost in the wind
Blind in the dust
Rocks in his hand
But, she knows wassup.
Made of glass
Dried up grass
What's growing overseas,
If I can't see me?
See me,
I need to see,
    Vividly.

It's a glass house, and she's on the outside
Throwing sand, cause I.
I've been standing tall through the storm
I've been in my element, shape shifting form.
I've been overcoming, and my enemies torn
Currently, abandonment and hate is the norm
I remember going hungry until Noon
Momma said, she'll be back soon
But soon wasn't quick enough
I learned patience when love got tough.

What is love? Who deserves it?
Who can I trust? How do I trust?
I am a savage when he's not looking,
Turning the scale in my favor
But you love to savor
Memories of her, AND I.

Love is the trustee
And my language is the beneficiary
Let us put the beef through THE machine...

I've lost a few
Who am I kidding?
I have lost many.
I've listened to women lie.
Then, Wept,
Die to themselves
Give their all
Just to ride by themselves.
Well, it's her call.
I've played it safe, by loving to a degree
Just to keep my sanity free.
Now I've paid the price.
Watching others blossom
Holding on to friendships by a hair
Standing in my kitchen thinking
Damn, this isn't fair.
I thought I was being honest enough
Loving enough
Trying enough
But when it comes to love
There will never be
Enough.
That's what I learned when love was lost.
Now we are in each other's DM.
My intuition tells me
You only contacted me because the elder
Of our connection
Detected, that together we could be a power house
Where was your compassion for me?
When I loved you, I made no decisions for you?
When I judged you, it was only to help you..
Besides, you asked me to. Alone now, let me be in my solitude.

"Developing the self to be sufficient,
is essential to our journey."

— Monique Rebel Jones —

"Determined to be in unity with the one I love. Unified by action seems to be the only way to love."

— Monique Rebel Jones —

Can you help me imagine?
I haven't known it all, to see it all.
Can you help me imagine?
I've been looking for the waves of hope
While being tossed around
Diving in and pouring out.

Can you help me imagine?
What my life could be if I just set myself free?
Free of comparisons.
Free from the doubt.
Free from the conversation going on inside
I'm convinced, I am too brave to hide
I am too resilient to show off my pride.
Yet, these words become too heavy to hold.
I'm doing my best to remain open.
Like a napkin, every end is centering.

Can you help me imagine?
How tall could I be?
How quick I can set myself free
Can you help me imagine,
How far could I go?
Based off what I could know
When I choose to grow
& let go
Could you
Would you
Help me imagine,
What my life could be, if I always chose me?
If I believed that I was worth being chosen?

What would life be if I had my basic needs met?
Imaginable.

Finally, I found the smile, I lost to the wind, now the oceans falling from the sky
Unwind my soul
So we could finally,
Live again
Because I don't want to die to you again
•

Earl was the name
He played silly games
Never knew the earth was a dome
Now he's programmed into the chrome

Searching for a lover

But he's really looking for his mother
Living a false narrative
Choking on his laxative

Yeah
Let it down
Let it...all down
Let the o-c-e-a-n fal-l dow-n
On, me

Cause finally...
I found the smile
I lost in the wind

365 DEGREES

The only thing sitting on my vertebrae,
Are the words I heard him say
You're a queen
And I don't receive that lightly.
Born with a gift
Now my synapses move swiftly.
I post one video real calm
Then, my prodigys bring on the storm
Like Venus on her axis
I'm about to have you all spinning backwards.
Retrograde so you can keep up,
Dusty colonizers, we're about to sweep up
Chiefs stand up
Cause once it's up
Ain't no way to keep up.
Light year mama with the double horn
Lover boys feeling torn
Torn between their childhood and the man I can make them become
Like the Messiah
I'm gonna rise, and still make you wait for me to come.
I drop one, then they drop two
What does that tell you?
You see me as your double
I see you wanting to start trouble
Yet, I'm too cool
To play a fool.
You know I do this for mi agente!
Dipped my toes in and became presidente!
Produced your finest,
And then you let me go, I do it all with no experience, CALL it growth.

Always giving my girls their flowers
I spent days putting in the work, more than just hours
I poured my love on them as needed, like sun showers.
My crown only tilted because I wanted it to be ours.
Yea, How many you know would share the throne, no publicity?
How many you know hold their shadows by the hand, tenacity?
Now you have the audacity,
To keep your lips tight, chastity.
Like a comet, I coming your way
Crashing into you, because my words have something to say.
Sick to the bone
The phony baloneys call themselve organic
But their trapped between the OMMM
I'm bringing all the souls home.
Rebel, against all odds
Call it devilish, but everyone has demons
I seem to be the only who knows the meaning
Even God has workers without a Will...
So I use mines, to produce a chill,
Power to Kill
Let the mercy be the skill
I am God choosing to feel.
Now, let me get my fire back
Seven years, and that of which no longer serves me has deserted me.
What seems like absence,
Is the presence of something new.
Always knew, pain would be the reason why
we grew.
Yea, we grew.

Time lapse through the winter
Pain under my skin like a splinter
Breaking the roots to the damned
Oh, but how could I love the fruit
Of which I am
Cut from the same tree
Hung over the matter of which another tree hates me?
They say it isn't personal
I think they lack imagination

Imagine we were merely God's resignation.
Resigning from our will
Giving power to the ill
Maybe God pity the creation
That was under his resting tone
Conceived under his restful damnation.
Wicked is the soil
that tumbled across this seed
In this seed was a miraculous new breed
awaiting to crack the past of its shell
At first it felt like a heated pillow
smothering the oxygen.
It encapsulated its veins into the past,
but that seed knew . . .
One day it'll grow plenty of fruit,
Therefore it grew.

Cycles transmute my paradigm
Into phases of my prime
unclothe my definition of love
symbols of peace
 create labyrinths in me.
Blinded as the light overlaying the layers of darkness
I will be like the rising sun seed
Pushing against the moist soil I call life.
With gradient meanings and probable connections
To minerals I call absent obstacles
Forcing my hand to be present
I capture my sprout as the moon absorbs
The matter of my plasma,
My heart like the nearest star to my womb
Elements of growth evolves outside the self
Elements of death diminishes cells
As I rebuild ETHER, thought, into Man.
A man into many.

She thought a million times she could dead it
But it was dead when she pulled it from the hands of death
Eternal life is the equation of breath
So
She
Recall the lies its tongue conjured before her eyes opened.
Premeditated assault to her feelings
No insult to injury while she's healing, please!
She wipes the grease off her pussy
Memories deleting from her bank of purpose
She is the chosen, one, two, three, four!
No more re-writing history.
It's time to give the enemy a hysterectomy...
Hand it to its face
Charmed with grace
Like, look what you made her do!
The strings attached to her emotions
Destroy her.
Giving the cosmic mother and father all the glory.
Said she wouldn't, then she did...
Destroyed herself when she realized what lies beneath the wig...lol

Unlearning the hole in the ground.
The tree in the hole.
The branch on the tree.
And how the green grass grows all around.
Unlearning the lullabies
That appeared to be an exit strategy
out of one scene
into the next.
I have watered my wounds with others' blood.
I have nurtured the dissociative attachment style
With ghosting.
Disappearing like the gardener
 tending to other areas of the garden,
I have become a seed again.
Growing,
This time knowing I am the seed.
This time knowing I have to blossom.
This time, knowing that time is for me to control.
This time, knowing that not knowing is a super power
 for those unlearning.
I need it.
I need, so often, I need.
Ever so often, I need, but this time
I am the gardener,
The seed,
The sun
The water,
The dirt..
And I am conscious of it all.
I am learning to enjoy the process.

Unstrip me of the minerals of my father.
I reek of his depression.
Unstrip me of the minerals of my mother,
I reek of her confidence.
Unstrip me of my arrogance
As I stand tall in my reason for being right when I am wrong.
Unstrip me of reason for causing others pain.
Unstrip my wounds
Let the sun draw out the myelin in my skin.
Protect me from myself.

PROCESS

DEAR GOD,

GAME OVER.
WAKE UP.
WAKE UP.

WHAT AM I TO DO?

CHILDREN ARE DYING OVER LAND.

WHY DID YOU SEND THEM HERE TO US?

I DON'T BELIEVE THIS. . . THIS MYTHICAL GOD.

I BELIEVE YOU ARE LIVING.

WHAT SHOULD I DO WITH MY BACHELORS DEGREE IN PSYCHOLOGY?
HOW AM I SUPPOSED TO HELP?
WHAT AM I TO DO ?

WHAT THE FUCKKKKK!!!!!!!!!!!!!!!!!!!!!!!!!!!!!!

WHAT TALENT DO I HAVE?
WHY IS IT SUCH A DIFFICULT THING FOR ME TO DO, TO JUST WRITE AND BE HEARD?

I DON'T WANT FAME, I WANT TO HEAL AND GROW AND PLANT FRUITFUL SEEDS IN THE MINDS OF THE PEOPLE.

I WANT TO GO HOME. I WANT TO BE CLOSE TO MY COSMIC MOTHER AND FATHER. I WANT TO GO HOME. HELP US ALL.

Weakness, in me?
Nah,
Not at all.
That could not be.
I am angry as fuck !
Sometimes, none of this makes sense.
Sometimes none of this is sensible.
Sometimes, I wonder did they pump me
Full of vaccines to slow me down,
Why would doctors do that?
Why do people agree to be part of something that would kill them
Eventually?

WHY, GOD?
Why?

God?
God?
What are you?
When are you?
Why are you?
Where ARE YOU!!!!???

Dancing in the street of gratitude
Between Malcom X and Fortitude.
I thought I knew it all, about my needs and
Then, the world fell on my lap
I had to lift it up, past my chin,
keep my pride inside
pretend I had nothing to HIDE.
It was the truth, in me,
the truth that would release me.

However, what did I know about living outside the bounds>
I'd rather beat my drum in silence,
Society noise can be violent.

My pride to be. . .
Discovering new versions of me,
They say do it anyway

Find out where the path that leads ASTRAY will bring you anyway.
I still don't trust it.

I've been on the narrow for a while, seems like I've circled the land
About a million times, probably led by my past life there.
Recycling generations of fear.
That's why I don't see them here.
Everyone is so grateful for me, yet, when will I be the one to believe,
and see just how great life jewels could be?

WHAT DO YOU DO FOR A LIVING?
I THINK THE REAL QUESTION IS,
WHO ARE YOU LIVING FOR?
WHO ARE YOU TODAY?
TODAY?
TODAY, I AM MOTHER.
"MOTHER, CAN YOU MAKE ME A SNACK?"
"MOTHER, CAN YOU HELP ME WASH UP?"
"MOTHER, CAN YOU PLAY WITH ME?"
"MOTHER, CAN YOU WASH MY HAIR?"
"MOTHER, HE HIT ME, CAN YOU MAKE HIM STOP?"

INTERRUPTED BY A PHONE CALL
I TAKE THE OPPORTUNITY TO STALL.

CLIENT: REBEL, CAN YOU SEND OUT THE EMAIL TO OUR LEAD?

SURE, THAT'S WHAT MOTHER'S DO.

The wings of my clitoris ✱
A head on collision with my destiny
Sensations at an all time high
This glory was meant to be.
I just stepped in a landfill of possibilities
Quantifying
No more denying
I accept im in control of my mind
My freedom has always been mine
I choose to thrive.
I have chosen to thrive.

A head on collision with my generational curse
Really a bag lady with a hearse
Call me Mary Poppins
The way I dig 6 ft in my 2 inches
Are you reading this?
I've been through my own version of the trenches
Always in the field
Never on the benches
They tell me rest
I ask my peers, is that a test>
I'll rest, when I'm 32000 feet in the sky
Bury me as star seed
Until then, I'm going to live
Until I die again. . .

My cranium pushing through the portal
Of pleasure
How could I ever measure, the amount of pressure
You would experience
Just for my existence
Although, I managed to push through
The challenges your decisions have presented.

They say it's a gift to be alive.
But if your energy is low
Then, BOOM
Existential crisis
I ponder if I might just..
 peel the crust from an eyelid
Feelings in the bottle
Processing feelings
Is like getting wifi in the desert for me.

What is it like for you?

Death of..
The ego...
The lack of security
The lack of thinking lack was the way to be
Humble has tumbled me and dried my imagination
Humbleness has defeated my every hope of being great.
The judgment I found on my tombstone read
I was once born, then I died to live again,
Again, I died while recollecting my strength to let go
What if ?
What if I fall asleep so deep into life,
I BECOME the visual, sensual being
That I would enjoy seeing.
What If I could fly instead of falling?
What if I became the void and life fell into me>
What if I became death itself?
Reminding life to keep on thriving.
Dancing in the rain
Reborn through the fire
I attest to the new version of my highest, most balanced identity,
I release the shackles of grief, fear, despair, and complacency
into the light.
Into the light.
Into the light.
Transcending the perspective that consciousness has formulated.
Into the light.

Su Ra talked about the body bags,
Horror stories, and the oppressors glory
About hate
Conditioned our young spongebobs
To think death was a sooner than later fate.
Rags to riches
What a drag?
But we voguing as if the war isn't happening
This is the shining
The plot twist, is the internal drainage
Brought on by radical change
For a radical frame
What is the name of the game, if all we do is place blame?
Being black was supposed to be an opposition
But we turn opposition into opportunity
No more cells, only immunity
Give me a boost of truth
Or else I'll pull up with a noose
Only to remind you, that the only inanimate object hanging from my neck
Are the symbols of my resurrection
Excessive obsessions turned into a docile erection
I can't get it up
May be if I make em' stuck
He would be willing not to give a fuck.

Can't close my eyes
This lifestyle is so dry.
Sand paper as my eyelids
Construction paper as my lips.
As I enter the dome, from the silicone
I scroll my eyes around the dimension of crystals
They call themselves human.

Hue of man
Man is weak.
Man is what man says.
Man is the dimension of flexible density.
Let us learn a lot, and throw all of it away.
We finally found our match
We finally found a fire I did not have to patch.

Finite is the dome.
All the way from silicone.

All these walls surrounding me
I feel like I can't breathe.
If you were to release me
I wouldn't know where to start my life,
Is it mine anyway?
Is it?
Yea?
Is it mine anyway?
These days, the Gods shake my world
Shape my pearls
So much information
So much dictation.
Plagiarism from the plagiarized
They frame my mind
to believe I was on the outside.
Three dimensional slide from the charts to the moon.
I was floating until I realized
My actual size.
I am larger than my name
As long as I adjust my frame!
Is it mine anyway?

Tender to the touch
My infant desires to be sati.
Tender to my finger tip,
slide down the slope,
I hope you like the dip.
I needed it, pleasure.
Pleasure
Due to the pain, I needed pleasure.
Oh, Pleasure,
Oh, pain.
Like a needle to an infant's arm
It's abnormal to feel your tools all over my body
I want the pain!
PLEASURE PLEASURE
PAIN, PAIN
PLEASURE !
ALL ON MY pain.

He was a stallion
I was a filly.
He was riding down the meadow,
Above the heads of many people
We don't know.
Yet, they were there
They were there.
We would ride into the sun rise
Never questioned who we were.
The wind was fine.
He was beautifully imperfect.
Life had left its mark on his loin.
He taught me how to ride.
He saw what I could become
From filly to a mare
He would not dare
Foal me as filly
But we wanted to touch
I thought I loved him so much.
He would listen
But I wouldn't dare
Show him the slope until I was a mare
He was my stallion.
He was my first ride into the sunrise.
Sunrise,
SUNrise.

Incapable of loving,
Because no man in my cipher showed us how to.
Men were all cutouts of a magazine
Faces from places.
However, I never knew where we were going.
Never knew this was telling.
Thought we were just displaying
No affection.
A good time, for a short time.
I forgot the time.

Incapable of loving him,
The way his mother used to.
So what do you need from me?
I only have one pussy,
Do you need me to be your visual star?
Oncall?
Or how about nonverbal on-call.
I just need to know?
A man's fantasy is based on his insecurities.
So, what's it going to be?

Your index arouses my intimate folds.
I reflect on how you should know what you want.
Where do you want it?
How long do you want it for>details.

I COMFORTABLY TALK TO EVERYONE ELSE BUT HIM.
I COMFORTABLY DANCE IN FRONT OF THE WORLD KNOWING I AM A MUSE
WITH HIM, I FEEL INSANELY OBJECTIONABLE.
I CAN WRITE PARAGRAPHS OF HOW I FEEL TO STRANGERS OF MY HEART COMFORTABLY
YET WITH HIM, IT IS AS THOUGH I'M WRITING A TERM PAPER & I AM DESPERATELY HOPING TO GET AN APPROVAL FROM HIM.
THOUGH YOU MIGHT NOT SEE THIS AS A CHALLENGE,
THE RHYTHM OF A HEARTBEAT
CAN TRULY FEEL LIKE A LACK OF HEAT?

Exposed brick sitting at the cerebellum of my medulla
Capsulated in the frame of my hope.
What is the frequency of love if love is a word described and not felt?
Felt but not heard?
Seen, yet experienced as layers of loss.
Exposed brick sitting at the layer of skin.
I wear my heart on my fingertips
Full of care
But so temperamental, I would dribble my own
If the game amused my impulsive nature.

Exposed brick on the inside
Chipped wood as the frame
Empty in the parameters of my image
Full in silence.

Exposed like an oversaturated image at noon.
No softener to change the scent of my dark shadows.
Exposed like the cowboy on forty-second street
Lights of sensual illusion. Exposed brick . . .
Tough to get through,
still, beautiful to frame for an image.

"A STORY WITHOUT A MIDDLE IS A STORY UNWRITTEN."

– MONIQUE OYO (11/4/23) –

www.ingramcontent.com/pod-product-compliance
Lightning Source LLC
Chambersburg PA
CBHW042310150426
43198CB00001B/27